CHINESE LOVE POEMS

If love be true, white hair still is black.
If there be no affection, even beauty falls into contempt.

ANCIENT SAYING

CHINESE
LOVE
POEMS

EDITED BY D. J. KLEMER

ILLUSTRATED BY SEONG MOY

DOUBLEDAY & COMPANY, INC., GARDEN CITY, NEW YORK

The editor and publisher are grateful to the following publishers and individuals for permission to include in this volume the selections listed below:

Harold Acton for his translation, in collaboration with Ch'en Shih Hsiang, of "The Unrequited Lover" from the book *From the Chinese*, edited by R. C. Trevelyan.

George Allen & Unwin, Ltd. (London) for selections from *Flower Shadows*, translated by Alan Lee Simms: "The Jewel," "Ancient Saying," "Ancient Poem."

Ch'u Ta'kao for his translation of selections from *Chinese Lyrics* with preface by Sir Arthur Quiller-Couch: "Her Birthday," "You and I," "A River-Long Love," "For Remembrance," "The Tryst."

E. P. Dutton & Co., Inc. for selections from *The Works of Li Po, the Chinese Poet*, done into English verse by Shigeyoshi Obata; copyright, 1922, by E. P. Dutton & Co., Inc.; renewal, 1950, by E. P. Dutton & Co., Inc.: "The Women of Yueh—IV," "Lines," "Maid of Wu," "To His Wife on His Departure—III," "By the Great Wall—II," "The Crows at Nightfall," "An Encounter in the Field."
From *Images in Jade*, translated by Arthur Christy; copyright, 1929, by E. P. Dutton & Co., Inc.; renewal, 1957, by Arthur E. Christy: "Spring Thoughts" and "Hearing a Flute on a Spring Night."

Houghton Mifflin Company for selections from *Fir Flower Tablets*, Poems translated from the Chinese by Florence Ayscough, English versions by Amy Lowell; copyright, 1921, by Florence Ayscough and Amy Lowell: "A Song of Grief," "The Lonely Wife," "After Being Separated for a Long Time," "Ai Ai Thinks of the Man She Loves," "The Blossoms of Lo Yang" ("Ch'n, the Fire-Bird with Plumage White as Jade Longs for Her Lover" and "Sent to Her Lover Yuan at Ho Han-South of the River"), "The Mirror" ("Written in the Character of a Beautiful Woman Grieving Before Her Mirror"), "Songs to the Peonies," "Song of the Courtesans," "Spring Grief and Resentment."

Bernhard Karlgren (Sweden) for selections from *The Book of Odes*, Chinese text, transcription, and translation by Bernhard Karlgren: "Wind and Violent Weather" (There is wind indeed . . .), "The Ten Acres" (Inside the ten acres . . .), "We Achieve Our Joy" (We achieve our joy in the stream-valley . . .), "Forsworn" (On the dykes there are magpies' nests . . .), "The Mulberry Trees" (The mulberry trees of the lowlands . . .), "The Stirred Waters" (In the stirred waters . . .), "That Crafty Youth" (That crafty youth, he does not talk . . .).

Alfred A. Knopf, Inc. for selections from *The Jade Mountain*, translated by Witter Bynner; copyright, 1929, by Alfred A. Knopf, Inc.: "Looking at the Moon and Thinking of One Far Away," "A Spring Sigh," "A Song of a Pure-Hearted Girl," "An Elegy," "Endless Yearning," "On Hearing Her Play the Harp," "On a Moonlight Night," "She Sighs on Her Jade Lute," "A Sigh from a Staircase of Jade," "The Garden of the Golden Valley," "To One Unnamed," "A Bitter Love," "Spring Heart-Break," "Alone in Her Beauty," "Spring Rain," "To One Unnamed."

Alfred A. Knopf, Inc. (New York) and George Allen & Unwin, Ltd. (London) for selections from *Translations from the Chinese* by Arthur Waley; copyright, 1919, 1941, by Alfred A. Knopf, Inc.: "Plucking the Rushes," "Five 'Tzu-Yeh' Songs," "Song of Snow-White Heads," "The Ferry," "Ch'n Chia's Wife's Reply," "South of the Great Sea," "The Little Lady of Ch'ing-Hsi," "Ch'n Chia's Farewell" ("Ch'n Chia"), "People Hide Their Love."

Mrs. R. Crowdy Mathers and Mrs. Marianne Rodker (London) for selections from *Lotus and Chrysanthemum*, translated by E. Powys Mathers; copyright, 1921, by Boni & Liveright, Inc.: "The White Frost" and "A Morning Shower."

Mosher Press (Portland, Maine) for selections from *Tu-Fu: Wanderer and Minstrel Under Moons of Cathay*, translated by Edna Worthley Underwood and Chi Hwang Chu: "The Love of a King" and "The Bride's Song."

John Murray, Ltd. (London) for selections from *300 Poems of the T'ang Dynasty*, translated by Soame Jenyns (which book appears in the Wisdom of the East series, distributed in America by the Grove Press): "Bestowed in Farewell," "A Ballad of Ch'ang Kan," and "Melancholy" (When you said you were coming . . .).

CONTENTS

PREFACE

Chinese tradition is at least 1000 years older than our own, and centuries ago cultivated Chinese had reached a degree of intellectual development that was quite remarkable even when interpreted by modern standards. These people were sophisticates.

Down through history the Chinese have looked upon poetry as a natural and solacing part of life. Of all the arts they felt it to be the most personal, for it alone requires no special accouterments like the canvases or stringed instruments of painting and music. It is solely dependent upon man's memory, and is carried about in his heart. Through the centuries almost everyone wrote verse—magistrates, scholars, cabinet ministers, emperors, courtesans, and housewives. Their poetry ran the gamut of situations experienced in everyday life. There are rollicking drinking songs, epics recording battles and political upheavals, laments for the dead, and many poems about love in all its moods. Many of the verses were intended to be sung—especially those from the BOOK OF ODES, a collection made by Confucius from the folk songs current in his day.

Until very recently Chinese society was such that woman's place was truly in the home. Marriages were generally arranged through a third party, between families, and without the consent of the betrothed; courtship was unknown. Thus, romantic love as we know it between engaged couples was almost nonexistent. On the other hand, nearly all ladies of letters were courtesans, and it was to them that men (poets included) turned for companionship and for entertainment. It is not surprising, therefore, that most of the love poetry of China dwells either on the growth of attachment after marriage, or on illicit love. Such poems as "The Fisherman" and "A Ballad of Ch'ang Kan" tell of married love. They are tender, dignified, entirely proper. Since the so-called romantic love affairs were almost always illicit, it is not surprising that the poetry commemorating them is of an entirely different nature. It was the clandestine meetings with their concubines that the poets praised in such frankly sensual verses as "People Hide Their Love" and "An Encounter in the Field." These are passionate and provocative.

Like today, early China had its share of wars and political difficulties. Civil servants and soldiers were frequently involved in frontier campaigns, long journeys, and banishment, and, as a result, perhaps half the poems in the Chinese language are poems of parting or separation. Husbands and wives—and lovers—tearfully bade one another good-by, and touchingly recorded their heartaches of farewell in poems like "A Farewell to My Love." The periods of separation often stretched into years and the persons involved spoke of the changing of the seasons, nights spent alone, the longing for loved ones, and boredom, unrelieved even by wine.

Whereas great attention has been paid to poetry throughout Chinese history, the golden age of Chinese poetry occurred during the T'ang Dynasty, between the years of 618 and 906 A.D. The heights attained by the poets in this three-hundred-year span was comparable to the accomplishments of painters and sculptors during the European Renaissance. This period had the usual preponderance of government officials among its roster of poets (like Prince Li Yü, who wrote "The Tryst," and like Po Chü-i, a cabinet minister, and the author of "Farewell in Secret"), but it was also an age of professional poets whom the emperors and statesmen recognized and honored. Li Po (705?–762?), the court poet of his day, was referred to as the genie of poetry. He was famous for his love of wine, women, and good fellowship. A generous sampling of his warm and engaging verse has been included here. Tu Fu (713–770) has been compared with Baudelaire. By nature he was frequently irascible and ill-tempered, but he was also possessed of an extraordinary tenderness and sympathy and it was these traits that dominated his poetry. Wang Wei (699–759), in addition to being another of the foremost poets of this period, was a great painter, a high official, and a philosopher.

While almost half of the verses in this collection were written by T'ang poets, most of the other dynasties are represented. As a guide to the reader the following list of these periods and their dates has been included:

> The Chou Dynasty 1121–256 B.C.
> The Ch'in Dynasty 255 B.C.–206 A.D.
> The Han Dynasty A.D. 206–221
> Period of Travail A.D. 222–618
> > *The Three Kingdoms Period* A.D. *222–264*
> > *The Chin Dynasty* A.D. *265–419*
> > *Southern and Northern Dynasties* A.D. *420–588*
> > *The Sui Dynasty* A.D. *589–617*
> The T'ang Dynasty A.D. 618–907
> The Five Dynasties A.D. 907–959
> The Sung Dynasty A.D. 960–1280
> The Yuan or Mongol Dynasty A.D. 1280–1368
> The Ming Dynasty A.D. 1368–1644
> The Ch'ing or Manchu Dynasty A.D. 1644–1911

The poems in this volume are by many different poets—some of whom have long since lost their identity—and include the best efforts of a variety of translators. Even after as many as 1700 years these verses remain vital, human and appealing, full of richness, warmth, and color. Many are sensuous; others tell of bitterness, loneliness, suffering, and grief. All are justified in taking their place beside the love poetry of today.

D. J. Klemer

come to

my arms . . .

FAREWELL IN SECRET

There can be no tears
For a secret farewell;
There can be no converse
For a hidden love.
Besides our two hearts no man can know it:
Locked deep in its cage by night the lonely bird rests;
The keen sword in Spring sunders the twining branches.
The water of the river, though muddy, may yet become clear;
The head of the crow, though black, may yet become white.
But for a secret farewell and for a hidden love,
The two must be content to hope for naught to come.

PO CHÜ-I
T'ANG DYNASTY

THE TRYST

The flowers bright, the moon dim, and a light mist eddying about—
Tonight is meant for me to go to my love.
Off with my stockings, I walk down the fragrant steps,
With my gold-lined slippers in hand.

At the south side of the Painted Hall we meet;
I fall trembling in his arms and say:
"Because it was so hard to come to you,
Let me have your very best caress."

PRINCE LI YÜ
T'ANG DYNASTY

THE FIFTH WATCH OF THE NIGHT

Look, my love!
The waning moon
Still sheds its fading light.
Do you hear that frightened bird
Calling for the dawn?
How mournful is its cry,
How lonesome for its nest
And mate!
Not yet, my own!
Cling to me,
Close to my heart.
I cannot let you go!

CHIEN T'ANG
CH'ING DYNASTY

TRAVELING

The red has parted from the green.
I'm half sober from my drink last night.
The horse in harness waits outside the door.
Fading bells without the house,
Fading candles before the curtains,
Fading moon beside the window.

She must be sleepless on her embroidered pillows,
Remembering that now the traveler has departed.
So hard to dismiss it from the heart,
So hard to see it,
So hard to speak it.

CHU TUN-RU
SUNG DYNASTY

FOR REMEMBRANCE

From the sun-touched hills the mists begin to withdraw,
In the clearing sky the scattered stars look fewer;
The sinking moon still shines on the faces of the lovers
Who are shedding tears at parting in the early morning.

Much has been said,
Yet we have not come to the end of our feelings.
Looking back she says again:
"If you remember my silken skirt of green,
Have tender regard for the sweet grass wherever you go."

NIU HSI-CHI
T'ANG DYNASTY

INCENSE AND MOONLIGHT

Like a great wheel
The brilliant moon
Gleams on the silken screen.
The bluish smoke curls slowly up
From the golden incense bowl
And scents the sweet warm air.
The wind
Brings the far-flung notes of a song,
Played on a flute of jade.

This autumn night
Our hearts are one,
Though our paths lie far apart.

KAN JU YÜ
CH'ING DYNASTY

PEOPLE HIDE THEIR LOVE

Who says
That it's by my desire,
This separation, this living so far from you?
My dress still smells of the lavender you gave:
My hand still holds the letter that you sent.
Round my waist I wear a double sash:
I dream that it binds us both with a same-heart knot.
Did not you know that people hide their love,
Like the flower that seems too precious to be picked?

WU-TI
HAN DYNASTY

Come to my chamber when you will,
My lord!
I await you with a longing
As ardent as your own.

A SONG OF CHERRY-TIME

A SONG OF CHERRY-TIME

My heart is stirred to its depths
By the fan that you have sent
To remind me of our love.

Come to my chamber when you will,
My lord!
I await you with a longing
As ardent as your own.

TZU YEH

CHIN DYNASTY

WAITING

I stand and watch
The moonlight creep
Through the great gate
Across the court.
I cannot sleep!

A stir in the night!
Is it you, my lord,
Come to my arms at last?

Ah!
'Tis but the shadow
Of dancing flowers,
High on the garden wall.—
And still I watch
And wait!

TS'UI YING YING

T'ANG DYNASTY

MEMORIES

I recall the time
I met you on the stair,
And the grief and pain
When parting came—too soon.
The world was well lost to you and me
When—so long ago!—
We met and parted on the stair.

I recall the time
I saw you slim and fair
Seated by the swaying curtains
Of soft silk.
You sang for me
Four or five sweet songs,
And played upon
Your murmuring lute.
Ah, there was nothing to compare
With your gentle smile,
As you sat and played and sang
For me alone.

I recall the time
We shared our evening meal,
And you sat silent, blushing deeply,
By my side.
You hardly touched your lips
To food or drink;
Your tiny mouth seemed
To need no bread nor meat.
Your slender hands were
Lilies white and fair,
When you sat with me
And shared my cup of wine.

I recall the tíme
You closed your eyes in sleep.
Late it was,
And all the world had gone to rest.
You removed your filmy silken robe
With no urging, no request—
Save from my eyes.
Timid, trembling,
You lay upon your bed—
I had to draw you, shrinking,
To my side.
You blushed and feared
To face the candle's light.

SHÊN YO
LIANG DYNASTY

TO ONE UNNAMED

A faint phœnix-tail gauze, fragrant and doubled,
Lines your green canopy, closed for the night. . . .
Will your shy face peer round a moon-shaped fan,
And your voice be heard hushing the rattle of my carriage?
It is quiet and quiet where your gold lamp dies,
How far can a pomegranate-blossom whisper?
. . . I will tether my horse to a river willow
And wait for the will of the southwest wind.

There are many curtains in your care-free house,
Where rapture lasts the whole night long.
. . . What are the lives of angels but dreams
If they take no lovers into their rooms?
. . . Storms are ravishing the nut-horns,
Moon-dew sweetening cinnamon-leaves—
I know well enough naught can come of this union,
Yet how it serves to ease my heart!

LI SHANG-YIN
T'ANG DYNASTY

A LETTER

Pearls!
Twin pearls,
Bright gems of ocean,
To me, a married woman,
You have sent!

Yet you know I have a husband
In attendance, in the palace,
On the Lord of Light, the Emperor—
May he live ten thousand years!

But the thought that prompted you
I cherish
In my bosom with the jewels.
There they've lain hidden till this hour,
In the soft, enfolding silk.

I know—you need not tell me—
That your thoughts are pure as moonlight,
Or as the glowing sun at midday
Overhead.

My home lies noble in its gardens.
There the marriage oath I've taken,
And I ever shall be faithful,
Even past the gates of death.
So!—
The twin pearls are in this letter.
I send them back to you in sadness
With a sigh.

If you look closely, you'll find with them
Two other twin gems lying,
Twin tears fallen from my eyelids,
Telling of a breaking heart.

Alas, that perverse life so willed it
That we met too late, after
I had crossed my husband's threshold
On that fateful wedding day!

CHANG CHI
T'ANG DYNASTY

JUST SIXTEEN

Standing there
In the flickering candle light,
Freed from your silken robes,
You are more beautiful than precious jade,
And more fragrant than those orchids
Beside your ivory bed.

With such charm of face and form
Who can believe
That you have spent these long spring months
Alone?

HSÜ CHIEN
CH'ING DYNASTY

SONG OF SONGS

I feast my eyes upon you
As you lie
With arms outstretched
Upon your couch.
Your hair, undone,
Flows down in shining waves
Upon your snow-white breast.

O my love!
There is no part of you
That does not stir
The swift and flaming passion
Of my love.

TZU YEH
CHIN DYNASTY

MAID OF WU

Wine of the grapes,
Goblets of gold—
And a pretty maid of Wu—
She comes on pony-back: she is fifteen.
Blue-painted eyebrows—
Shoes of pink brocade—
Inarticulate speech—
But she sings bewitchingly well.
So feasting at the table
Inlaid with tortoise shell,
She gets drunk in my lap.
Ah, child, what caresses
Behind lily-broidered curtains!

LI PO
T'ANG DYNASTY

SONG OF THE RIVER

My boat is of ebony;
the holes in my flute are golden.

As a plant takes out stains from silk,
so wine takes sadness from the heart.

When one has good wine,
a graceful boat,
and a maiden's love,
why envy the immortal gods?

LI PO
T'ANG DYNASTY

THE SHORELESS SEA

Oh dragon,
you who rule the shoreless sea of death,
steal away my loved one
while, bending over her in passionate musing,
I drink in her breath,
bear her away on your ghostly ship,
and take me with her
so we may sail together always,
drunk with love.

LI HUNG-CHANG
CH'ING DYNASTY

YOU AND I

You and I
Love each other so
As from the same lump of clay
Is moulded an image of you
And one of me.
In a moment of ecstasy
We dash the images to pieces,
Put them in water,
And with stirring and kneading
Mould again an image of you
And another of me.
There and then,
You will find yourself in me,
I myself in you.

KUAN TAO-SHÊNG
SUNG DYNASTY

FIVE SONGS

At the time when blossoms
Fall from the cherry-tree:
On a day when yellow birds
Hovered in the branches—
You said you must stop,
Because your horse was tired:
I said I must go,
Because my silkworms were hungry.

All night I could not sleep
Because of the moonlight on my bed.
I kept on hearing a voice calling:
Out of Nowhere, Nothing answered "yes."

I will carry my coat and not put on my belt;
With unpainted eyebrows I will stand at the front window.
My tiresome petticoat keeps on flapping about;
If it opens a little, I shall blame the spring wind.

I heard my love was going to Yang-chou
And went with him as far as Ch'u-shan.
For a moment when you held me fast in your outstretched arms
I thought the river stood still and did not flow.

I have brought my pillow and am lying at the northern window,
So come to me and play with me awhile.
With so much quarrelling and so few kisses
How long do you think our love can last?

TZU YEH

CHIN DYNASTY

24

A MORNING SHOWER

The young lady shows like a thing of light
In the shadowy deeps of a fair window
Grown round with flowers.

She is naked and leans forward, and her flesh like frost
Gathers the light beyond the stone brim.

Only the hair made ready for the day
Suggests the charm of modern fashion.

Her blond eyebrows are the shape of very young moons.

The shower's bright water overflows
In a pure rain.

She lifts one arm into an urgent line,
Cooling her rose fingers
On the gray metal of the spray.

If I could choose my service, I would be the shower
Dashing over her in the sunlight.

J. S. LING
CH'ING DYNASTY

NOONDAY

I think
I never loved her more than now,
As she lies asleep at noonday
On her couch.

There she is,
Beautiful to behold,
Her fan fallen from her tiny hand,
Her great golden pins
Thrust loosely through her hair.
The yellow lilies
And the pines
Appear to shrink and turn away,
As though fearing
To disturb her blessèd sleep.

While I?—
I gently reach out a stealthy hand,
To span the length
Of her tiny silken shoe.

FAN TSENG HSIANG
CH'ING DYNASTY

THE GARDEN OF THE GOLDEN VALLEY

Stories of passion make sweet dust,
Calm water, grasses unconcerned.
At sunset, when birds cry in the wind,
Petals are falling like a girl's robe long ago.

TU MU
T'ANG DYNASTY

sweet words
that touch
the ear . . .

HER BIRTHDAY

A feast being spread in spring-time,
With a cup of green wine and a joyous song.
I repeat my salutation and offer my three wishes:
First, may you have a long life;
Second, may I have good health;
Third, may we live as the swallows on the beam,
Happily together all the year round.

FÊNG YEN-CHI
T'ANG DYNASTY

YOUTH

Who can see her
And not love her?
Pure and sweet
In the first blush of youth,
She is bright and fair
As the blossoms of spring,
And her name
Is Hsiao Ku Tzu.

TZU YEH
CHIN DYNASTY

THE SMALL BOY

The small boy
Is sitting outside the door on the stone-seat
And weeping and wailing he wants to have a wife
When he has got a wife what will he do with her?
When the lamp is lighted he will have a chat with her
When the lamp is out he will keep company with her
And the next morning after getting up she will comb his small pigtail.

A SMALL GIRL

A door of the temple is opposite to a door of the temple
There lives a small girl
With white cheeks
And red lips
She walks so nicely that she makes people die of love.

ASH TREES

Ash trees, ash trees—
Under the ash trees they have raised a stage
Everybody's girls are come
Only mine does not come yet
Just while speaking, here she is come
Riding on a donkey
With an open parasol
And with her hair combed into a chignon.

THE FERRY

Of marsh-mallows my boat is made,
The ropes are lily-roots.
The pole-star is athwart the sky:
The moon sinks low.
It's at the ferry I'm plucking lilies,
But it might be the Yellow River—
So afraid you seem of the wind and waves,
So long you tarry at the crossing.

EMPEROR CH'IEN WĒN-TI
LIANG DYNASTY

THE WOMEN OF YUEH

She, a Tung-yang girl, stands barefoot on the bank,
He, a boatman of Kuei-chi, is in his boat.
The moon has not set.
They look at each other—broken-hearted.

LI PO
T'ANG DYNASTY

A POEM FOR WANG LUNG

Li Po was about to sail in his boat,
When suddenly he heard sounds of stamping and singing on shore.
The Peach Flower Lake is a thousand fathoms deep,
But it cannot compare with Wang Lung's love, bidding farewell.

LI PO
T'ANG DYNASTY

A RIVER-LONG LOVE

I live at the upper end of the River,
And at the lower end live you;
Every day I long to see you but cannot,
Though from the same River we drink.

When will the River go dry?
When can my sorrow come to an end?
Only may your heart be like mine,
My love for you will not be in vain.

LI CHIH-YI

SUNG DYNASTY

AT THE RIVER'S EDGE

At the river's edge
maidens are bathing among the water-lilies;
they are hidden from the shore,
but their laughter can be heard,
and on the bank
their silken robes perfume the wind.

A youth on horseback passes near;
one of the maidens feels her heart beat faster,
and she blushes deeply.

Then she hides herself
among the clustered water-lilies.

LI PO

T'ANG DYNASTY

THE WILLOW LEAF

The maiden who gazes dreamily from her window
resting on her elbows,—
I do not love her for her splendid palace
on the banks of the Yellow River;
I love her
because she has dropped a little willow leaf
into the water.

I do not love the breeze from the east
because it brings me
the scent of the blossoming peach trees
that whiten the Oriental Mountain;
I love it
because it has blown the little willow
leaf close to my boat.

And the little willow leaf,—
I do not love it for reminding me
of the tender spring
that has just flowered again;
I love it
because the maiden has written a name on it
with the point of her embroidery needle,
and because that name is mine.

TCHAN TIOU-LIN

THE AUTUMN WIND

The autumn wind rises,
white clouds are flying before it,
yellow leaves are torn from the trees
by the river.

Will your shy face peer round a moon-shaped fan,
And your voice be heard hushing the rattle of my carriage?

TO ONE UNNAMED

Already the wild geese are winging their way
towards the south,
the rose is sweet no longer,
and petals are falling
from the lotus flowers.

I must see her whom I love
and can never forget;
I jump into my boat
to cross the river to the pavilion
where she dwells.

The stream is swift
and the waters,
darkened by the wind,
flow with a sound like rustling silk;
how far away seems the other shore,
as far away as ever!

To give me courage
I sing as I row,
but my songs are sad
and make my toil heavier.

My heart is young and ardent;
it flies before me
and pitilessly leaves me.

Have the winds of so many autumns
broken my strength?
Is it the image of an old man
that trembles up at me
from the water?

EMPEROR OU-TY

HAN DYNASTY

THE BLOSSOMS OF LO YANG

I

My Lover is like the tree-peony of Lo Yang.
I, unworthy, like the common willows of Wu Ch'ang.
Both places love the Spring wind.
When shall we hold each other's hands again?

II

Incessant the buzzing of insects beyond the orchid curtain.
The moon flings slanting shadows from the pepper-trees across the courtyard.
Pity the girl of the flowery house,
Who is not equal to the blossoms
Of Lo Yang.

TING LIU NIANG
LIANG DYNASTY

SONG OF THE COURTESANS

My skirt is cut out of peacock silk,
Red and green shine together, they are also opposed.
It dazzles like the gold-chequered skin of the scaly dragon.
Clearly so odd and lovely a thing must be admired.
My Lord himself knows well the size.
I beg thee, my Lover, give me a girdle.

TING LIU NIANG
LIANG DYNASTY

THE UNREQUITED LOVER

I fancy that I'm an unrequited lover
But I know not whom I love.
Maybe a land in faint haze by the sea,
Maybe a flower withering in silence,
Maybe some beauty met on a road and then forgotten:
I cannot tell.
As if I were in love
My bosom swells, my heart throbs ever faster.
Tired, I would wander through dark streets,
Wander through all riotous places
And think not to return, as if in search of something.
A floating pin-point of bewitching eye,
Sweet words that touch the ear—
Such incidents are common;
But I would say in a low voice: "Not you!"
And stagger on elsewhere.

'Night-walker' people call me.
Let them!—it's all the same to me.
In sooth I am a lonely night-walker,
A lover unrequited.

T'AI WANG-SHU
CH'ING DYNASTY

ON HEARING HER PLAY THE HARP

Her hands of white jade by a window of snow
Are glimmering on a golden-fretted harp—
And to draw the quick eye of Chou Yü,
She touches a wrong note now and then.

LI TÜAN
T'ANG DYNASTY

SONGS TO THE PEONIES

I

The many-coloured clouds make me think of her upper garments, of her lower garments;
Flowers make me think of her face.
The Spring wind brushes the blossoms against the balustrade,
In the heavy dew they are bright and tinted diversely.
If it were not on the Heaped Jade Mountain that I saw her,
I must have met her at the Green Jasper Terrace, or encountered her by accident in the moon.

II

A branch of opulent, beautiful flowers, sweet-scented under frozen dew.
No love-night like that on the Sorceress Mountain for these; their bowels ache in vain.
Pray may I ask who, in the Palace of Han, is her equal?
Even the "Flying Swallow" is to be pitied, since she must rely upon ever new adornments.

III

The renowned flower, and she of a loveliness to overthrow Kingdoms—both give happiness.
Each receives a smile from the Prince when he looks at them.
The Spring wind alone can understand and explain the boundless jealousy of the flower,
Leaning over the railing of the balcony at the North side of the aloe-wood pavilion.

LI PO
T'ANG DYNASTY

THE LOVE OF A KING

He sits upon gold that glows—the Son of Heaven.
His noble courtiers resemble heaped gems.
He is Heaven—with moon, with the stars!

His counselors speak gravely.
They discuss worlds; they discuss wars.

The Emperor does not hear.
His thoughts are a bird that has spread its wings to be free.

In an ivory tower—one gorgeous-hued flower, the Empress.
Women resplendent in silks surround her.

My love is away too long!
She sighs.
Her fan grows languid.

Perfume caresses the Emperor's face.
The Sweet One sends me the scent of her lips!

A rainbow of gems, the Emperor, enters the Tower.

War counselors stare at each other.
They are useless now.
They are silent.

They know not love!

TU FU
T'ANG DYNASTY

PLUCKING THE RUSHES

Green rushes with red shoots,
Long leaves bending to the wind—
You and I in the same boat
Plucking rushes at the Five Lakes.
We started at dawn from the orchid-island:
We rested under the elms till noon.
You and I plucking rushes
Had not plucked a handful when night came!

POET UNKNOWN
PERIOD OF TRAVAIL

AN ENCOUNTER IN THE FIELD

Came an amorous rider,
Trampling the fallen flowers of the road.
The dangling end of his crop
Brushes a passing carriage of five-colored clouds.
The jeweled curtain is raised,
A beautiful woman smiles within—
"That is my house," she whispers,
Pointing to a pink house beyond.

LI PO
T'ANG DYNASTY

a pinch

of ashes . . .

MELANCHOLY

When you said you were coming it was but empty words;
Now that you have gone you have left no trace.
The moon shines aslant the roofs at the fifth watch;
I dream that you have gone away for good;
I cry out, but it is impossible to call you back.
I try to write to you, but such is my haste that the ink is not properly mixed.
On the top part of the cage the light of the wax lanterns reflects the gold king-
    fisher feathers.
The musk perfume floats faintly through the embroidered hibiscus curtains.
Liu was sorry that Paradise was so far away,
But I am still more troubled, for I am much further away than he.
The east wind comes in gusts, bringing soft drops of rain;
Beyond the hibiscus pond there is faint thunder.
The gold toad bites on the lock and the incense comes through;
The jade tiger pulls at the rope and the water is drawn up from the well.
The lady Chia spied through the screen on the charms of the young secretary
    Han;
The lady Mi left a pillow for the prince of Wêi,
But the human heart in spring cannot hope to vie with the flowers,
For every surge of heart there is a pinch of ashes.

LI SHANG-YIN
T'ANG DYNASTY

THE LITTLE LADY OF CH'ING-HSI

Her door opened on the white water
Close by the side of the timber bridge:
That's where the little lady lived
All alone without a lover.

A CHILDREN'S SONG

ALONE IN HER BEAUTY

Who is lovelier than she?
Yet she lives alone in an empty valley.
She tells me she came from a good family
Which is humbled now into the dust.
. . . When trouble arose in the Kuan district,
Her brothers and close kin were killed.
What use were their high offices,
Not even shielding their own lives?—
The world has but scorn for adversity;
Hope goes out, like the light of a candle.
Her husband, with a vagrant heart,
Seeks a new face like a new piece of jade;
And when morning-glories furl at night
And mandarin-ducks lie side by side,
All he can see is the smile of the new love,
While the old love weeps unheard.
The brook was pure in its mountain source,
But away from the mountain its waters darken.
. . . Waiting for her maid to come from selling pearls
For straw to cover the roof again,
She picks a few flowers, no longer for her hair,
And lets pine-needles fall through her fingers,
And, forgetting her thin silk sleeve and the cold,
She leans in the sunset by a tall bamboo.

TU FU
T'ANG DYNASTY

THE LANTERN FESTIVAL

Last year at the Lantern Festival
The flower-market lights were bright as day;
When the moon mounted to the tops of the willows,
Two lovers kept their tryst after the yellow dusk.

This year at the Lantern Festival
The moon and the lights are the same as then;
Only I see not my lover of yesteryear,
And tears drench the sleeves of my green gown.

OUYANG HSIU
SUNG DYNASTY

A SONG OF GRIEF

Glazed silk, newly cut, smooth, glittering, white,
As white, as clear, even as frost and snow.
Perfectly fashioned into a fan,
Round, round, like the brilliant moon,
Treasured in my Lord's sleeve, taken out, put in—
Wave it, shake it, and a little wind flies from it.
How often I fear the Autumn Season's coming
And the fierce, cold wind which scatters the blazing heat.
Discarded, passed by, laid in a box alone;
Such a little time, and the thing of love cast off.

PAN CHIEH-YU
HAN DYNASTY

THE JEWEL

On my flute of ebony I played to you the most impassioned
songs that I know, but your eyes followed the flight
of pigeons and you would not listen.

I gave you a poem in which I praised your beauty, but you tore it up,
throwing the pieces on the waters of the lake, because, as you said,
there were no lotus petals.

I would have given you a wondrous jewel, limpid and cold as a Winter's
night, but I keep it because it is like your heart.

WAN TSE

LOVE

Lingering, lingering,
Pulsating, pulsating
Two hearts beat in one.
Fine as gossamer,
Vast as the waves,
Inconstant as the moon,
Frail as a flower,
This strange thing we call love,
What a prolific source of sorrows it is!

WU YUNG
T'ANG DYNASTY

THE LEAF ON THE WATER

The wind tears a leaf from the willow tree;
it falls lightly upon the water,
and the waves carry it away.

Time has gradually effaced a memory from my heart,
and I watch the willow leaf drifting away on the waves;
since I have forgotten her
whom I loved,
I dream the day through in sadness,
lying at the water's edge.

But the willow leaf floated back
under the tree,
and it seemed to me
that the memory could never be effaced
from my heart.

OUAN-TSI

THE WHITE FROST

The white frost covers all the arbute-trees
Like powder on the faces of women.

Looking from my window I consider
That a man without women
Is like a flower—naked without its leaves.

To drive away my bitterness
I write this thought with my narrow breath
On the white frost.

WANG CHI
T'ANG DYNASTY

SOUTH OF THE GREAT SEA

My love is living
To the south of the Great Sea.
What shall I send to greet him?
Two pearls and a comb of tortoise-shell:
I'll send them to him packed in a box of jade.
They tell me he is not true:
They tell me he dashed my box to the ground,
Dashed it to the ground and burnt it
And scattered its ashes to the wind.
From this day to the ends of time
I must never think of him,
Never again think of him.
The cocks are crowing,
And the dogs are barking—
My brother and his wife will soon know.
The autumn wind is blowing;
The morning wind is sighing.
In a moment the sun will rise in the east
And then *it* too will know.

POET UNKNOWN

A BITTER LOVE

How beautiful she looks, opening the pearly casement,
And how quiet she leans, and how troubled her brow is!
You may see the tears now, bright on her cheek,
But not the man she so bitterly loves.

LI PO
T'ANG DYNASTY

SONG OF SNOW-WHITE HEADS

Our love was pure
As the snow on the mountains:
White as a moon
Between the clouds—
They're telling me
Your thoughts are double:
That's why I've come
To break it off.
Today we'll drink
A cup of wine.
Tomorrow we'll part
Beside the Canal:
Walking about,
Beside the Canal,
Where its branches divide
East and west.
Alas and alas,
And again alas.
So must a girl
Cry when she's married,
If she find not a man
Of single heart,
Who will not leave her
Till her hair is white.

CHO WĒN-CHŪN
HAN DYNASTY

DEATH OF LOVE

But yesterday
I loved,
And life was sweet.
I loved,
And my spirit soared
To heights undreamed.

Today
The sun in vain
Shines on a darkened life,
A spirit pale and dead—
For love is done!

POET UNKNOWN

CHIN DYNASTY

HEARING A FLUTE ON A SPRING NIGHT

From whose flute, playing in some hidden place, come those flying notes,
Which the Spring wind wafts over the town?
The melody is that of the Willow Song.
Who can hear it and not think of his former loves?

LI PO

T'ANG DYNASTY

ny eyes upon you
ie
ns outstretched
ur couch.

SONG OF SONGS

THROUGH YOUR WINDOW

I watched your red lips move
In song,
And your jade-like fingers pluck
The stringèd lute.

Love urged me on—
To enter,
Take you in my arms,
Make you my own.

But I blushed, I trembled,
I dared not move—
And now
It is too late!

TZU YEH

CHIN DYNASTY

A PEASANT SONG

Before the door
Stands a jujube tree.
It has been there so many years
That it does not know
Its age.

How can the old woman
Ever hope
To hold a grandchild
In her arms
When she has never even
Tried to find
A husband for her girl?

POET UNKNOWN

LIANG DYNASTY

48

I feast
As you
With a
Upon

DEATH OF LOVE

But yesterday
I loved,
And life was sweet.
I loved,
And my spirit soared
To heights undreamed.

Today
The sun in vain
Shines on a darkened life,
A spirit pale and dead—
For love is done!

POET UNKNOWN
CHIN DYNASTY

HEARING A FLUTE ON A SPRING NIGHT

From whose flute, playing in some hidden place, come those flying notes,
Which the Spring wind wafts over the town?
The melody is that of the Willow Song.
Who can hear it and not think of his former loves?

LI PO
T'ANG DYNASTY

THROUGH YOUR WINDOW

I watched your red lips move
In song,
And your jade-like fingers pluck
The stringèd lute.

Love urged me on—
To enter,
Take you in my arms,
Make you my own.

But I blushed, I trembled,
I dared not move—
And now
It is too late!

TZU YEH
CHIN DYNASTY

A PEASANT SONG

Before the door
Stands a jujube tree.
It has been there so many years
That it does not know
Its age.

How can the old woman
Ever hope
To hold a grandchild
In her arms
When she has never even
Tried to find
A husband for her girl?

POET UNKNOWN
LIANG DYNASTY

I feast my eyes upon you
As you lie
With arms outstretched
Upon your couch.

SONG OF SONGS

like

a swallow

to its mate . . .

THE FISHERMAN

The earth has drunk the snow,
and now the plum trees are blossoming once more.

The willow leaves are like new gold;
the lake is molten silver.

It is the hour
when sulphur-laden butterflies
rest their velvet heads upon the flowers.

A fisherman casts forth his nets
from a motionless boat,
and the surface of the lake is broken.

His thoughts are at home with her
to whom he will return with food,
like a swallow to its mate.

LI PO
T'ANG DYNASTY

A SONG OF A PURE-HEARTED GIRL

Lakka-trees ripen two by two
And mandarin-ducks die side by side.
If a true-hearted girl will love only her husband,
In a life as faithfully lived as theirs,
What troubling wave can arrive to vex
A spirit like water in a timeless well?

MÊNG CHIAO
T'ANG DYNASTY

THE BRIDE'S SONG

The bean-vine twines around the hemp-stalk.
It twists and twists but it never grows long.

A girl married to an enlisted soldier is poorer than the beggar who sits by the
    road.
Married at night, parted at dawn.

You say you do not go far.
But you go to Ho-Yian!

When I lived with my father and mother they did not let a man look at me.
Now they have flung me away!

And now you go to the battle!

I swore I would follow.
You were unhappy and suffered.

Now I say this to you:
Go! Be brave!
I shall not follow the army.
That is not for a woman.

But I do regret I made so many wedding dresses.
How can I wear them?
Watch me wash off the powder, the paint!
Now you need not worry.

TU FU
T'ANG DYNASTY

CH'IN CHIA'S FAREWELL

Solemn, solemn the coachman gets ready to go:
"Chiang, chiang" the harness bells ring.
At break of dawn I must start on my long journey:
At cock-crow I must gird on my belt.
I turn back and look at the empty room:
For a moment I almost think I see you there.
One parting, but ten thousand regrets:
As I take my seat, my heart is unquiet.
What shall I do to tell you all my thoughts?
How can I let you know of all my love?
Precious hairpins make the head to shine
And bright mirrors can reflect beauty.
Fragrant herbs banish evil smells
And the scholar's harp has a clear note.
The man in the Book of Odes who was given a quince
Wanted to pay it back with diamonds and rubies.
When I think of all the things you have done for me,
How ashamed I am to have done so little for you!
Although I know that it is a poor return,
All I can give you is this description of my feelings.

CH'IN CHIA
HAN DYNASTY

CH'IN CHIA'S WIFE'S REPLY

My poor body is alas unworthy:
I was ill when first you brought me home.
Limp and weary in the house—
Time passed and I got no better.
We could hardly ever see each other:
I could not serve you as I ought.
Then you received the Imperial Mandate:
You were ordered to go far away to the City.
Long, long must be our parting:
I was not destined to tell you my thoughts.
I stood on tiptoe gazing into the distance,
Interminably gazing at the road that had taken you.
With thoughts of you my mind is obsessed:
In my dreams I see the light of your face.
Now you are started on your long journey
Each day brings you further from me.
Oh that I had a bird's wings
And high flying could follow you.
Long I sob and long I cry:
The tears fall down and wet my skirt.

HAN DYNASTY

A SOLDIER'S WIFE TO HER HUSBAND

If duty to your country means
That you must die
And return to our parent earth
On the far-off north frontier,
Know
That my love for you shall be
As strong and imperishable
As that stone
Upon the mountain side.

LIU CHI
MING DYNASTY

ON A MOONLIGHT NIGHT

Far off in Fu-chou she is watching the moonlight,
Watching it alone from the window of her chamber—
For our boy and girl, poor little babes,
Are too young to know where the Capital is.
Her cloudy hair is sweet with mist,
Her jade-white shoulder is cold in the moon.
. . . When shall we lie again, with no more tears,
Watching this bright light on our screen?

TU FU
T'ANG DYNASTY

FROM EXILE

Today carries me back
A long, long year.
Again I feel you
Clinging to my sleeve,
And our children
Tugging at my knees
In last farewell.

Tonight
I am alone,
Save where,
In the dying lamplight,
Restless shadows
Move and creep,
And in the dreary watches
Of the night
No one ever comes
To talk of home.

HSÜ CHU

CH'ING DYNASTY

TO HIS WIFE ON HIS DEPARTURE

Gold are the staircases, and like a kingfisher's wings
Sparkle the towers of the house where I shall be.
But the thought of you, my dear, who will stand alone
By the ancient gate and weep,
Will make me sit awake at night by the lonely lamp,
And watch the dying moon of dawn;
And all my tears shall flow as I journey on to the west.

LI PO

T'ANG DYNASTY

A BALLAD OF CH'ANG KAN

PART I

In the days when my hair first fell over my forehead
And in play I plucked flowers before the door,
You came riding to me on a bamboo horse.
Throwing blue plums, we chased each other round the bed.
Together we lived in the hamlet of Ch'ang Kan,
In those days we were both young and innocent.
At the age of fourteen I became your wife.
So bashful that I dared not look up,
I hung my head in the darkest corners.
A thousand times you called me, but I did not answer.
At the age of fifteen I began to come to my senses
And plighted my troth to you till we should be dust and ashes together.
We kept faith as he who clung to the poet of old.
How should I dally on the tower seeking a husband's return?
When I was sixteen you went on a far journey.
In the gorges of Ch'u Tang foaming rapids defy the traveller.
In the fifth month they cannot be passed in safety.
The monkeys lift their melancholy howls in the distant heights.
Before the door I gaze where your parting feet have trodden.
Little by little the green moss covers them,
Deep green moss that cannot be brushed away.
Already the leaves are falling in the autumn wind.
In the eighth month the yellow butterflies come;
They flutter in pairs over the flowers of the western garden.
These matters touch my heart with emotion
As I sit lonely while my bloom fades to age.
Sooner or later you must return down the Three Gorges.
Do not forget to send a letter informing me of your arrival,
Then I will meet you nor fear the distant road
Even to the Long Wind Beach.

PART II

I remember that when I lived in the depths of the women's apartments
I knew nothing of the dust and dirt of the outside world.
When I married the man from Ch'ang Kan
On the sandspit I used to watch the state of the wind,
In the fifth month the southern wind gets up,
And I used to think of you dropping down the river to Pa Ling.
In the eighth month the western wind rises,
And my heart would go out to you starting along the Yangtze.
I see you so little and you are so long away.
How many days will it take you to reach Hsiang T'an?
In my dreams I ride the wind-tossed waves:
Yesterday evening a cruel wind swept across the waters.
Its breath broke down the trees at the river mouth.
Wide, wide the dark expanse of water ruffled by the wind
And the traveller is swallowed up in it.
Oh that you could borrow a piebald steed from the floating clouds,
I would meet you east of the Orchis Island,
Just like the mandarin-duck and drake sitting beside green rushes,
Or a pair of kingfishers on an embroidered screen.
In self-pity I remember how, when I was little more than fifteen,
My complexion was red like peach blossom.
Who would be a merchant's wife?
Fearful of waters and winds alike.

LI PO
T'ANG DYNASTY

AN ELEGY

O youngest, best-loved daughter of Hsieh,
Who unluckily married this penniless scholar,
You patched my clothes from your own wicker basket,
And I coaxed off your hairpins of gold, to buy wine with;
For dinner we had to pick wild herbs—
And to use dry locust-leaves for our kindling.
. . . Today they are paying me a hundred thousand—
And all that I can bring to you is a temple sacrifice.

We joked, long ago, about one of us dying,
But suddenly, before my eyes, you are gone.
Almost all your clothes have been given away;
Your needlework is sealed, I dare not look at it. . . .
I continue your bounty to our men and our maids—
Sometimes, in a dream, I bring you gifts.
. . . This is a sorrow that all mankind must know—
But not as those know it who have been poor together.

I sit here alone, mourning for us both.
How many years do I lack now of my threescore and ten?
There have been better men than I to whom heaven denied a son,
There was a poet better than I whose dead wife could not hear him.
What have I to hope for in the darkness of our tomb?
You and I had little faith in a meeting after death—
Yet my open eyes can see all night
That lifelong trouble of your brow.

YÜAN CHÊN
T'ANG DYNASTY

AFTER SEEING HER IN A DREAM

Her floating life vanished like a bubble.
Cruel Fate nipped the frail flower too soon!
I brood over her memory, and cannot forget
How we blew at the showers of roses together,
When she had done with her needlework;
How we leaned cheek to cheek upon the secluded balustrade,
Watching the sunset.

The happy dream cannot be prolonged.
The unfinished poem will never be continued.
A bitter weeping at midnight is all my gain.
Her image is still vivid in my mind,
But her soul comes and goes like the wind,
Eluding the embrace of man!

She must now be threading her way to the azure through the maze of space;
Her short hair must have caught some frost in the dawning air.
Though she is in heaven and I on earth,
Our Karma ties have not altogether snapped!
Before the Spring flowers and the Autumn moon,
Our inner chords are touched and sadness fills our hearts.
But the more we yearn to renew our union,
The more we shudder at our separateness!
A pair of love-birds have been torn apart,
To bleed in two different worlds from the same wound!
Ah, what agony!
The dreary sound of the rain dripping from the eaves
Is music to the coils of my sorrowing bowels!

NALAN HSINTEH
CH'ING DYNASTY

THE MIRROR

I

Bright, bright, the gilded magpie mirror,
Absolutely perfect in front of me on the jade dressing-stand.
Wiped, rubbed, splendid as the Winter moon;
Its light and brilliance, how clear and round!
The rose-red face is older than it was yesterday,
The hair is whiter than it was last year.
The white-lead powder is neglected,
It is useless to look into the mirror. I am utterly miserable.

II

When my Lord went away, he gave me this precious mirror coiled with dragons
That I might gaze at my golden-threaded dress of silken gauze.
Again and again I take my red sleeve and polish the bright moon,
Because I love to see its splendor lighting up everything.
In its center is my reflection, and the golden magpie which does not fly away.
I sit at my dressing-stand, and I am like the green Fire-Bird who, thinking of
its mate, died alone.
My husband is parted from me as an arrow from the bow-string.
I know the day he left; I do not know the year when he will return.
The cruel wind blows—truly the heart of the Unworthy One is cut to pieces.
My tears, like white jade chop-sticks, fall in a single piece before the water-
chestnut mirror.

LI PO
T'ANG DYNASTY

long,

long must be

our parting . . .

A FAREWELL TO MY LOVE

The shivering cicada wailed heart-rendingly.
A long road stretched out before me in the eventide.
A sudden shower had just stopped.
In the tent by the city gate, I drank farewell to my love in a gloomy mood.
Just where I wanted to linger a bit,
The boatman came to hasten my departure.
Her hands in mine, we gazed into each other's tear-filled eyes.
Mutely we gulped down our frozen sobs.
Ah, how many miles of mists and waves I have to travel through!
The boundless sky of Ch'u merged into the deepening shades of the night.
From of old, lovers have always suffered from separation.
But the pale, forlorn Autumn adds poignancy to my pain.
Awakening from my drunken sleep,
Where do I find myself tonight?
The shores are full of willows,
And the dawn breeze is rising and the moon is setting!
For a whole year I shall be away from her.
Henceforth, fair days and beautiful sceneries need not exist for me.
Who will be there
To share Romance with me?

LIU YUNG
SUNG DYNASTY

BESTOWED IN FAREWELL

PART I

She is slender and elegant and not yet fourteen,
Beautiful as the tips of the cardamum buds in early spring.
Although the spring wind may blow the whole length of the Yang Chou road,
When they roll up their beaded blinds there is none to be compared with her.

PART II

She has so much passion, yet tonight it would seem as if she had none.
Although we are drinking for the last time she fails to force a smile.
But the wax candles seem to understand and sorrow at our parting;
They deputize forces and they weep till early dawn.

TU MU
T'ANG DYNASTY

TO ONE UNNAMED

Time was long before I met her, but is longer since we parted,
And the east wind has arisen and a hundred flowers are gone;
And the silk-worms of spring will weave until they die
And every night the candles will weep their wicks away.
Mornings in her mirror she sees her hair-cloud changing,
Yet she dares the chill of moonlight with her evening song.
. . . It is not so very far to her Enchanted Mountain—
O blue-birds, be listening!—Bring me what she says!

LI SHANG-YIN
T'ANG DYNASTY

HAN POEM—IX

In the courtyard grows a rare tree
With green leaves and a splendid flowering.
Lifting myself to the branch, I cut down some blossoms;
I shall send them to him on whom my heart dwells.
The sweet smell fills my sleeves and lap.
The distance is too great for it ever to reach you.
Moreover, such a gift would hardly please you.
Now I know how long you have been away.

SPRING GRIEF AND RESENTMENT

There is a white horse with a gold bridle to the East of the Liao Sea.
Bed-curtains of open-work silk—embroidered quilt—I sleep with the Spring
    wind.
The setting moon drops level to the balcony, it spies upon me. The candle is
    burnt out.
A blown flower drifts in through the inner door—it mocks at the empty bed.

LI PO
T'ANG DYNASTY

She gets drunk in my lap.
Ah, child, what caresses
Behind lily-broidered curtains!

MAID OF WU

THE LONELY WIFE

The mist is thick. On the wide river, the water-plants float smoothly.
No letters come; none go.
There is only the moon, shining through the clouds of a hard, jade-green sky,
Looking down at us so far divided, so anxiously apart.
All day, going about my affairs, I suffer and grieve, and press the thought of
    you closely to my heart.
My eyebrows are locked in sorrow, I cannot separate them.
Nightly, nightly, I keep ready half the quilt,
And wait for the return of that divine dream which is my Lord.

Beneath the quilt of the Fire-Bird, on the bed of the Silver-Crested Love-
    Pheasant,
Nightly, nightly, I drowse alone.
The red candles in the silver candlesticks melt, and the wax runs from them,
As the tears of your so Unworthy One escape and continue constantly to flow.
A flower face endures but a short season,
Yet still he drifts along the river Hsiao and the river Hsiang.
As I toss on my pillow, I hear the cold, nostalgic sound of the water-clock:
Shêng! Shêng! it drips, cutting my heart in two.

I rise at dawn. In the Hall of Pictures
They come and tell me that the snow-flowers are falling.
The reed-blind is rolled high, and I gaze at the beautiful, glittering, primeval
    snow,
Whitening the distance, confusing the stone steps and the courtyard.
The air is filled with its shining, it blows far out like the smoke of a furnace.
The grass-blades are cold and white, like jade girdle pendants.
Surely the Immortals in Heaven must be crazy with wine to cause such disorder,
Seizing the white clouds, crumpling them up, destroying them.

LI PO
T'ANG DYNASTY

AFTER BEING SEPARATED FOR A LONG TIME

How many Springs have we been apart? You do not come home.
Five times have I seen the cherry-blossoms from the jade window,
Besides there are the "embroidered character letters."
You must sigh as you break the seals.
When this happens, the agony of my longing must stop your heart.
I have ceased to wear the cloud head-dress. I have stopped combing and dress-
     ing the green-black hair on my temples.
My sorrow is like a whirling gale—like a flurry of white snow.
Last year I sent a letter to the Hill of the Bright Ledge telling you these things;
The letter I send this year will again implore you.

East wind—Oh-h-h-h!
East wind, blow for me.
Make the floating cloud come Westward.
I wait his coming, and he does not come.
The fallen flower lies quietly, quietly, thrown upon the green moss.

LI PO
T'ANG DYNASTY

SPRING HEART-BREAK

With twilight passing her silken window,
She weeps alone in her chamber of gold;
For spring is departing from a desolate garden,
And a drift of pear-petals is closing a door.

LIU FANG-P'ING
T'ANG DYNASTY

GOOD NEWS

More than a year has passed
Since you and I
Parted in grief and tears.

Today at last
A letter came,
One tiny, narrow sheet.

Tonight I've lit my lamp
A hundred times
To read its words of love.

LIN I NING
CH'ING DYNASTY

SENT TO HOME

You ask when I shall come home.
There is no date yet.
Just now, here at Pa-shan,
Night rain is flooding the Autumn pools.

I look forward to the time
When we shall snuff the candle
Together by the western window,
And I shall tell you how I feel
This night at Pa-shan,
When the rain is flooding the Autumn pools.

LI SHANG-YIN
T'ANG DYNASTY

SONG FOR THE MOON ON MOUNT OMEI

Like a crescent of autumn shines the moon of Omei:
The pale light floods the Ping-chiang River.
Tonight I shall leave Ching-chi for the Three Gorges—
Then down to Yochow, thinking of you whom I cannot see!

LI PO
T'ANG DYNASTY

LONELY NIGHT IN EARLY AUTUMN

Thin leaves wave on the wu-t'ung tree beside the well.
Through the pounding of the washerwomen, autumn begins to sing.
Under the eaves, I find a place and sleep alone,
And waking, I see the bed half filled with the moon.

PO CHÜ-I
T'ANG DYNASTY

A GIRL'S YEARNING

One range of mountains,
Two ranges of mountains,
The mountains are far, the sky high, the mists and waters cold.
My lingering thoughts have reddened the maple leaves.

The chrysanthemums bloom,
The chrysanthemums wither.
The wild geese from the border fly high, but my love has not come home.
The wind and the moon play idly on the screen.

PRINCE LI YÜ
T'ANG DYNASTY

LINES

Cool is the autumn wind,
Clear the autumn moon,
The blown leaves heap up and scatter again;
A raven, cold-stricken, starts from his roost.
Where are you, beloved?—When shall I see you once more?
Ah, how my heart aches tonight—this hour!

LI PO
T'ANG DYNASTY

WAITING FOR NEWS

Since you left, I know not whether you are far or near,
I only know the colors of nature have paled and my heart is pent-up with
    infinite yearnings.
The more you travel, the farther you go and the fewer your letters.
The waters are broad, and the fish sink deep; where to find any news of you?

In the depth of night the wind plays on the bamboos an autumnal tune,
Echoed by the direful song of the endless leaves.
Leaning upon the single pillow, I try to conjure up the Land of Dreams where
    to seek for you.
Alas! no dreams come, only the dim lamplight fuses with the shadows!

OUYANG HSIU
SUNG DYNASTY

AI AI THINKS OF THE MAN SHE LOVES

How often must I pass the moonlight nights alone?
I gaze far—far—for the Seven Scents Chariot.
My girdle drops because my waist is shrunken.
The golden hairpins of my disordered head-dress are all askew.

TING LIU NIANG
LIANG DYNASTY

SHE SIGHS ON HER JADE LUTE

A cool-matted silvery bed; but no dreams. . . .
An evening sky as green as water, shadowed with tender clouds;
But far off over the southern rivers the calling of a wildgoose,
And here a twelve-story building, lonely under the moon.

WÊN T'ING-YUN
T'ANG DYNASTY

THINKING OF HER

Upon a high balcony I lean alone.
The silken wind blows mildly.
I strain my gaze afar.
The sorrow of separation oozes dimly from the horizon.
The color of the grass and the light of the mountains glimmer in the waning
    sun.
No one can divine the feelings that surge in my bosom.

I too have thought of drowning my sorrows in the ocean of wine,
And singing out the burden of my mind.
But forced joys leave no taste in the mouth.
What if my robe and girdle should grow looser every day?
Is it not for *her* that I am suffering?

LIU YUNG
SUNG DYNASTY

BOREDOM

We can sing a different tune from the "Song of Desolation?"
The wind is sighing!
The rain is sighing!
The roseate flower of the candle is wearing itself out for another night!

I know not what is tangling up the skein of my thought.
Sober, I am bored!
Drunk, I am bored!
Even dreams refuse to carry me to the neighborhood of my love!

NALAN HSINTEH
CH'ING DYNASTY

ENDLESS YEARNING

I

I am endlessly yearning
To be in Ch'ang-an.
. . . Insects hum of autumn by the gold brim of the well;
A thin frost glistens like little mirrors on my cold mat;
The high lantern flickers; and deeper grows my longing.
I lift the shade and, with many a sigh, gaze upon the moon,
Single as a flower, centered from the clouds.
Above, I see the blueness and deepness of sky.
Below, I see the greenness and the restlessness of water . . .
Heaven is high, earth wide; bitter between them flies my sorrow.
Can I dream through the gateway, over the mountain?
Endless longing
Breaks my heart.

II

The sun has set, and a mist is in the flowers;
And the moon grows very white and people sad and sleepless.
A Chao harp has just been laid mute on its phœnix-holder,
And a Shu lute begins to sound its mandarin-duck strings . . .
Since nobody can bear to you the burden of my song,
Would that it might follow the spring wind to Yen-jan Mountain.
I think of you far away, beyond the blue sky,
And my eyes that once were sparkling
Are now a well of tears.
. . . Oh, if ever you should doubt this aching of my heart,
Here in my bright mirror come back and look at me!

LI PO
T'ANG DYNASTY

YEARNINGS OF LOVE

The weather is getting cold.
The wine lies like poison on my heart.
On the window beats the rain.

The fading fragrance, like a little pupil,
Is simulating the feelings of Autumn.

"Cheer up, cheer up!" I said to my heart,
But tears have stolen into my blue gown.

Yearnings for my love keep me sober
In defiance of the wine.
I lie listlessly in my lonely bed.
I remember when I parted from her,
The peach-trees were flowering,
And the willows waving their tender locks.

NALAN HSINTEH
CH'ING DYNASTY

LOOKING AT THE MOON AND THINKING
OF ONE FAR AWAY

The moon, grown full now over the sea,
Brightening the whole of heaven,
Brings to separated hearts
The long thoughtfulness of night. . . .
It is no darker though I blow out my candle.
It is no warmer though I put on my coat.
So I leave my message with the moon
And turn to my bed, hoping for dreams.

CHANG CHIU-LING
T'ANG DYNASTY

THE CROWS AT NIGHTFALL

In the twilight of yellow clouds
The crows seek their nests by the city wall.
The crows are flying home cawing—
Cawing to one another in the tree-tops.
Lo, the maid of Chin-chuan at her loom
Weaving brocade,—for whom, I wonder?
She murmurs softly to herself
Behind the blue mist of gauze curtain.
She stops her shuttle, and broods sadly,
Remembering him who is far away—
She must lie alone in her bower at night,
And her tears fall like rain.

LI PO
T'ANG DYNASTY

THINKING OF MY LOVE

A tress of cloud!
A shuttle of jade!
A pale, pale robe of thin, thin gauze!
A nameless grace playing about her knitted brows
Like a faint shade!

Autumn gales start,
Echoed by the rain.
Outside the window screen
A pair of plantain-trees grow wide apart.
The long, long night wears out a longing heart.

PRINCE LI YÜ
T'ANG DYNASTY

74

ANCIENT POEM

Deep green lies the grass along the river.
Far away the road stretches, a road without end.
I dare not think of the endlessness of that road.

Last night I saw him in a dream.
In a dream I had him here beside me.
Suddenly I awoke to feel again his absence.
Far, far away is he in unknown lands.
I turn away, not daring to see his empty place.

The withered mulberry tree knows the bitterness of Heaven's cold.
Others are happy in the loves of their homes.
No one is there to talk with me.

From a far place there has come a guest.
He has brought me the present of a pair of carp.
I order the little boy to prepare them;
And in one of them he finds a strip of paper.
Kneeling down I read it.
The first line says:
"Cherish thyself for me,"
The second line says:
"Think of me always."

ANONYMOUS

A SIGH FROM A STAIRCASE OF JADE

Her jade-white staircase is cold with dew;
Her silk soles are wet, she lingered there so long . . .
Behind her closed casement, why is she still waiting,
Watching through its crystal pane the glow of the autumn moon?

LI PO
T'ANG DYNASTY

SPRING SORROW

In the grip of Spring sorrow,
Her soul has snapped asunder.
The fragrant grass cannot bear to see
The sweet season passing away.

The flowers fall noiselessly
In the twilight rain.
In a secluded mansion,
All alone she stands
Leaning against the door.

WEI CHUANG
T'ANG DYNASTY

BY THE GREAT WALL

He rides his white charger by the Fortalice of Gold,
She wanders in dreams amid the desert cloud and sand.
It is a season of sorrow that she scarce can endure,
Thinking of her soldier lover at the border fort.
The fireflies, flitting about, swarm at her window,
While the moon slowly passes over her solitary bower.
The leaves of the green paulonia are tattered;
And the branches of the sha-tung blasted and sere.
There is not an hour but she, alone, unseen,
Weeps—only to learn how futile all her tears are.

LI PO
T'ANG DYNASTY

SPRING THOUGHTS

The grass of Yen grows green and fine as silk;
Low hangs the mulberry branch in the state of Chin.
And in the remembering time of day my heart is broken,
For then I know you think of me.
O strange Spring wind, I know you not at all.
Why do you pass through the silken curtain of my bower?

LI PO
T'ANG DYNASTY

SPRING RAIN

I am lying in a white-lined coat while the spring approaches,
But am thinking only of the White Gate City where I cannot be.
. . . There are two red chambers fronting the cold, hidden by the rain,
And a lantern on a pearl screen swaying my lone heart homeward.
. . . The long road ahead will be full of new hardship,
With, late in the nights, brief intervals of dream.
Oh, to send you this message, this pair of jade earrings!—
I watch a lonely wild goose in three thousand miles of cloud.

LI SHANG-YIN
T'ANG DYNASTY

A SPRING SIGH

Drive the orioles away,
All their music from the trees. . . .
When she dreamed that she went to Liao-hsi Camp
To join him there, they wakened her.

CHIN CH'ANG-HSÜ
T'ANG DYNASTY

PARTING AND MEETING

She left her love
A young and red-cheeked girl.
When next they met,
Her hair was white.

Vanished
Was her beauty,
But the tears of parting
Still seemed to linger
In her eyes.

KAO SHIH
T'ANG DYNASTY

COCK-CROW

The cock has crowed, says the girl;
The day has broken, says the man.
Arise, observe the night!
Is it the stars that shine?
Quickly begone! Quickly begone!
To hunt the duck and the wild goose.

When thou hast killed I will prepare them
And we will feast on them.
And, as we feast, we will drink.
Oh, that with thee I might grow old.
Beside us are lutes and guitars:
Everything makes tranquil of our love.

If I were sure of thy coming,
I would give thee my trinkets.
If I were sure of thy favour,
I would send thee my trinkets.
If I were sure of thy love,
My trinkets should repay thee.

TUCKED-UP SKIRTS

If thou hast loving thoughts of me,
I will tuck up my skirts and cross the Chên.
But if thou hast no thoughts for me,
Are there, then, no other men?
Oh maddest of mad youths, in truth.

If thou hast loving thoughts of me,
I will tuck up my skirts and cross the Wei.
But if thou hast no thoughts for me,
Are there, then, no other boys?
Oh maddest of mad youths, in truth.

Upon a high balcony I lean alone.
The silken wind blows mildly.
I strain my gaze afar.

THINKING OF HER

THE EPHEMERA

Oh, the wings of the ephemera.
Oh, the beautiful, beautiful garment.
How sad am I at heart. . . .
Come thou and dwell with me.

Oh, the wings of the ephemera.
Oh, the fine many-colored robe.
How sad am I at heart. . . .
Come thou and rest with me.

It comes from the earth, the ephemera.
Hempen robe, white as snow.
How sad am I at heart. . . . '
Come thou and be happy with me.

THE QUINCE

He gave me a quince,
I gave him a jade pendant,
Not in repayment,
But to make our love lasting.

He gave me a peach,
I gave him an emerald,
Not in repayment,
But to make our love lasting.

He gave me a plum,
I gave him black jade,
Not in repayment,
But to make our love endure.

THE WHITE PONY

Pure is the white pony,
Feeding on the young shoots in my stackyard.
Keep him hobbled, keep him bridled,
Let him stay through all mornings.
So may my lover
Here take his ease.

Pure is the white pony,
Feeding on the bean sprouts in my stackyard.
Keep him hobbled, keep him bridled,
Let him stay through all evenings.
So may my lover
Here have his peace.

Pure is the white pony
Who comes to me swiftly,
Like a duke, like a marquis,
Let us enjoy ourselves completely,
Let us prolong our love-making,
Let us take our ease.

Pure is the white pony
Who lies in the empty valley
With a bundle of fresh hay.
He is like a piece of jade.
Oh, do not be like gold or jade.
Do not go far from my heart!

WE ACHIEVE OUR JOY

We achieve our joy in the stream-valley;
Oh, the grandeur of the stately man!
When separated from me he sleeps and wakes and talks,
Forever, he swears, he will not forget me.

We achieve our joy on the sloping hill;
Oh, the greatness of that stately man!
When separated from me he sleeps and wakes and talks,
Forever, he swears, he will not be unfaithful to me.

We achieve our joy on the high ground.
Oh, the prominence of the stately man!
When separated from me he sleeps and wakes and sojourns,
Forever, he swears, he will not tell of our love.

THE STIRRED WATERS

In the stirred waters the white stones are shining;
With white robe and red collar I follow you to Wu;
When I have seen my lord, how should I not be happy?

In the stirred waters the white stones are purely white;
With white robe and red embroidery I follow you to Hu;
When I have seen my lord, how should I be anxious?

In the stirred waters the white stones are fretted;
I have heard your summons;
I dare not tell people about it.

I PRAY THEE

I pray thee, Master Chung,
Leap not into my village.
Break not my willow-trees . . .
How should I dare to love thee? . . .
I am afraid of my parents . . .
Chung, I might love thee, indeed,
But my parents' words
Are also to be feared.

I pray thee, Master Chung,
Jump not over my wall.
Break not my mulberry-trees . . .
How should I dare to love thee? . . .
I am afraid of my cousin . . .
Chung, I might love thee, indeed,
But my cousin's words
Are also to be feared.

I pray thee, Master Chung,
Leap not into my orchard.
Break not my plants of t'an . . .
How should I dare to love thee?
I am afraid of the scandals . . .
Chung, I might love thee, indeed,
But the scandals which people talk
Are also to be feared.

THE TEN ACRES

Inside the ten acres, the pickers of mulberry-leaves are moving leisurely;
I will stroll and turn off with you.

Outside the ten acres, the pickers of mulberry-leaves are moving slowly;
I will stroll and go with you.

THE DEAD HIND

On the plain there is the dead hind;
With white grass wrap it round.
There is a girl dreaming of spring.
Good fellow, solicit her.

In the forest there are bushes;
On the plain there is the dead fawn.
With white grass wrap it round.
The girl is like a diamond.

Gently, gently; press me not.
Do not touch my girdle!
Whatever you do, do nothing
To cause my dog to bark.

THE RAINBOW

The rainbow is in the east.
None dare point to it.
The girl when she marries,
Leaves behind brothers and relatives.

Morning mist in the west.
It will rain all the morning.
The girl when she marries,
Leaves behind brothers and relatives.

Now the girl whom you see
Dreams of being married
Without further keeping her purity
And before the marriage has been arranged.

VILLAGE LOVES OUTSIDE THE GATE

Outside the east gate
The girls are like a cloud.
Although they seem a cloud
None holds my thought.
White robe and gray cap,
She it is who can delight me.

Beyond the bastion of the gate
The girls are like white flowers.
Although they are like white flowers
None fills my thoughts.
White robe and madder cap,
She it is who can charm me.

THE MODEST GIRL

The modest girl, how lovely.
She awaits me at the corner of the wall,
I love her, and, if I see her not,
I scratch my head, bewildered. . . .

The modest girl, how charming.
She gives me a red tube.
The red tube is brilliant;
The girl's beauty is enchanting.

Plant which comes from the meadows,
Truly as lovely as rare,
Nay, 'tis not thou that art lovely:
Thou art the gift of loveliness.

THE CHÊN

The Chên and the Wei
Have overflowed their banks.
The youths and maidens
Come to the orchids.
The girls invite the boys:
. . . Suppose we go over?
And the lads reply:
. . . Have we not been?
Even so, yet suppose
. . . we go over again.

For over the Wei
A fair greensward lies.
Then the lads and the girls
Take their pleasure together;
And the girls are then given
. . . a flower as a token.

The Chên and the Wei
Are full of clear water.
The lads and the girls invite
In crowds are assembled
The girls invite . . .

THAT CRAFTY YOUTH

That crafty youth, he does not talk with me!
Yes, it is all your fault, but it makes me unable to eat.

That crafty youth, he does not eat with me!
Yes, it is all your fault, but it makes me unable to rest.

THE MULBERRY TREES

The mulberry trees of the lowlands are beautiful, their leaves are ample;
When I have seen my lord, how great is the joy!

The mulberry trees of the lowlands are beautiful, their leaves are glossy;
When I have seen my lord, how should I not be happy!

The mulberry trees of the lowlands are beautiful, their leaves are dark;
When I have seen my lord, his fine reputation closely unites us.

In my heart I love him, why should I not tell it?
In the core of my heart I treasure him, when shall I forget him?

THE COCK CROWS

THE LADY: The cock has crowed.
           The sun has arisen.

THE LOVER: It is not yet cockcrow—
            Only the buzzing of the bluebottles.

THE LADY: The east is alight.
           The sun is aflame.

THE LOVER: It is not the dawn—
            Only the moon rising.

THE LADY: The bluebottles must be drowsy.
           It is sweet to lie by your side.

THE LOVER: Quick! Let me go from you.
            Do not let me hate you!

THE CHARIOT AXLES

With heavy blows I have made fast the axles of my chariot.
I go to find the fair young girl, the substance of my dreams.
What can hunger mean to me? What care I for thirst?
With her charm she is coming to me.
Although I have no good friends,
Yet come, let us feast and be merry.

In that thick forest on the plain,
The pheasants meet together.
At the proper time this noble girl
With her great virtue comes to help me.
Come then, let us feast and sing her praises.
I will love thee and never tire.

Although I lack delicate spirits,
Yet come, let us drink, I invite.
Although I have no dainty dishes,
Yet come, let us eat, I entreat.
Although my virtue does not equal yours,
Yet come, let us sing and then dance.

I climbed that lofty height
And there cut down branches of oak.
And there cut down branches of oak.
Their leafage how fresh and green.
What luck for me to unite with thee.
Ah, my heart, what comfort it knows.

The lofty heights may be admired;
The high roads may be traveled
My four horses how docile they are.
Their six reins suggest a lute.
I am joined with thee, my new-made bride,
And thus I set peace in my heart.

THE PEASANT

Oh, peasant who seemed quite simple,
Exchanging thy cloth for silken thread,
Thou camest not to get the silken thread:
Thou camest to inveigle me.
I followed thee over the Ch'i,
As far as the hill of Tuan . . .
"— 'Tis not I would postpone the time;
Thou hast no good go-between."
. . . "I pray thee be not angry.
Let autumn be the time."

I climbed upon that ruined wall
To look towards Fu Kuan . . .
Nothing in sight towards Fu Kuan . . .
My tears fell down like rain . . .
When I saw thee towards Fu Kuan
Ah, then I laughed and talked.
. . . "The tortoise and the milfoil
Foretell no ill for me."
. . . "Come then and bring thy carriage
My trousseau to convey."

When the mulberry sheds its leaves
They are tender to the touch. . . .
Alas, alas, O turtle-dove,
Eat not the mulberry fruits.
Alas, alas, O gentle girl,
With boys take not thy pleasure.
When a young man takes his pleasure,
He may be excused.
But when a girl takes pleasure,
There is no excuse.

When the mulberry sheds its leaves,
They fall, already yellow . . .
Since I came to live with you,
Three years have passed in poverty . . .
How high is the river Ch'i,
Wetting the carriage hangings . . .
The girl has never been forsworn.
The boy has played a double game.
The boy, 'tis true, has been unjust
Twice, thrice, he changed his mind.

For three years I have been thy wife,
Of toil I never wearied;
Early to rise and late to rest,
I never had a morning.
And as long as that endured
Thou didst treat me harshly . . .
My brothers, they shall never know.
They would laugh and mock me . . .
Quietly I ponder it
And hug my grief in secret!

Along with thee I would grow old,
And, old, thou hast made me suffer . . .
Yet the Ch'i has its banks . . .
Yet the valley has sides . . .
In my girlish head-dress thou didst feast me! . . .
Thy voice, thy laugh, they pleased me.
Thy vow was clear as the dawn.
I did not dream that thou wouldst change . . .
That thou wouldst change . . . I did not dream . . .
Now, it is finished . . . alas . . .

FORSWORN

On the dyke there are magpies' nests,
On the hill there are sweet t'iao plants;
Who has enticed my beautiful one?
In my heart I am pained.

On the temple path there are tiles,
On the hill there are sweet yi plants;
Who has enticed my beautiful one?
In my heart I am grieved.

THE BUNDLES OF FIREWOOD

I have bound in bundles the branches.
The three stars are in the sky.
Ah, what an evening is this one
On which I see thee my wife.
Alas for thee! Alas for thee!
With my wife, what shall I do?

WIND AND VIOLENT WEATHER

There is wind indeed and violent weather;
When you look at me, you smile, yet you ridicule me and treat me with laughing
    arrogance;
In the core of my heart I am grieved at this.

There is wind indeed and clouds of dust;
Kindly you promised to come, yet you do not frequent me;
Long brooding is my thinking.

There is wind indeed and wind-blown dark skies;
At every time of the day there are wind-blown dark skies; I keep awake and
    do not sleep;
While longing I am chagrined.

Caused by wind-blown skies is the cloudiness, the thunder;
I keep awake and do not sleep while longing,
I keep yearning for you.

Last night I saw him in a dream.
In a dream I had him here beside me.
ANCIENT POEM

She is naked and leans forward, and her flesh like frost
Gathers the light beyond the stone brim.

A MORNING SHOWER